*M*om, I have always kept
my feelings for you
in the most precious
place within me.

My memories of home
go with me wherever I go,
and they keep me
close to you.

And in all the days of my life,
from the most distant
yesterday
to the farthest tomorrow,
I know that I will never stop
thanking you
for everything you are to me
and for everything you do.

– Collin McCarty

I Love You,
Mom

A collection of poems
Edited by Gary Morris

Blue Mountain Press ®

Boulder, Colorado

ACKNOWLEDGMENTS appear on page 64.

Library of Congress Catalog Card Number: 98-30608
ISBN: 0-88396-475-9

 design on book cover is registered in the U.S. Patent and Trademark Office.

Manufactured in Singapore
First Printing: December 1998

Library of Congress Cataloging-in-Publication Data

I love you, mom : a collection of poems / edited by Gary Morris.
     p.   cm.
     ISBN 0-88396-475-9 (alk. paper)
     1. Mothers--Poetry. 2. American poetry--20th century.
I. Morris, Gary, 1958-
PS595.M64115 1998
811'.5080920431--dc21   98-30608
                                                   CIP

Blue Mountain Press®

P.O. Box 4549, Boulder, Colorado 80306

Table of Contents

Mom, If I Could, I'd Give You the World...

I wish I could build you that
dream home that you've always wanted.
I would fill it with your favorite people
and your happiest memories.

I wish I could take back all those times
when I hurt your feelings or let you down.
I would exchange them with words like,
"I love you" or "I'm so glad you're my mom."

I wish I could guarantee that we'd have
all the tomorrows we'd ever want,
and all the time we'd ever need to celebrate
and enjoy our great relationship.

But I can't build you your dream home
or change the past
or predict the future.

So I will just tell you how much I love
the person you are,
what an unforgettable, wonderful influence
you've had on my life,
and how very glad I am
that you're my mother.

– Debra Elliott

You Have Always
Been Everything to Me

You have been my teacher –
helping me to learn about life,
pointing me in the right direction,
letting me make my own mistakes
and then helping me pick up
   the pieces afterwards.
You have been my friend –
   listening to me when I needed to talk,
   making me talk when I didn't know
      I needed to,
   supporting me when I was down,
   and helping me to see that things
      weren't all that bad.
You have been my role model –
   leading me by your example.
Most of all, you have been my mother –
   loving me unconditionally
   no matter what I did or said,
   letting me know that I was not alone
      and never would be,
   for I would always have a home.

I can never thank you enough
  for all that you have taught me,
  given to me, and done for me.
I can never repay you.
All I can do is tell you
  that I love you with all my heart,
  that I'm grateful for you,
  and that I cherish you
  and the closeness we share.
I feel incredibly lucky
  to have been gifted
    with a mother like you.
      I love you.

– Deborah A. Brideau

A Mother's Love
Is One of a Kind

Only once in your life
will someone so special
walk in front of you
and prepare the way
for a better future.
Only once will there be a person
who cares enough to say "no,"
but is enthusiastic enough
to say "yes" whenever possible.
Only once in your life
will someone wait patiently
while you make
the most important decisions of your life.
Only once will you know someone
who has the courage not to back down
from a decision she's made.
Only once will you have the opportunity
to be loved by someone
who could never love you more
than she does every day.
A mother's love is one of a kind.

– Debbie Hearon

A Very Special Poem
for a Very Special Mom

*There are so many moments
when I wish you knew... how much you
matter to me, and how much I thank you
  for being such a wonderful mother.*

*If there is happiness in my heart,
  it's because you helped put it there.
If there is gentleness in my beliefs,
  it's because you showed me how to care.
If there is understanding in my thinking,
  it's because you shared your wisdom.
If there is a rainbow over my shoulder,
  it's because of your outlook and your vision.
If there is a knowledge that I can reach out –
  and I really can make some dreams come true –
  it's because I learned from the best
      teacher of all.
    I learned... from you.*

*In the times of my life, whether we
are near or far, please remember
that there could never be any mother
more wonderful... than the one you are.*

– Chris Gallatin

You've Done So Much for Me...

How Can I Ever Thank You?

Time and time again, you've read my heart, sensed my need, and gone out of your way to help me when you just as easily could have told me that I was on my own and no longer your concern.

Rather than lecture me, you listened, you advised, and you cautioned. Sometimes the differences between our generations hit head-on. Through it all, we both changed a little, though I know I had the most to learn and benefit from your guidance. You have taught me so much and sacrificed for me often. Even though I've told you before, I want to thank you again.

Life hasn't always been a "breeze" for me; you and I both know my weaknesses and my mistakes. I'm sorry if I've burdened you with my problems. Sometimes I don't know what I'd do without you.

I know it is blessed to give, but it is also blessed to receive. I just wish I could trade blessings with you now and let you be on the receiving end for a change.

I hope you can feel my gratitude and heartfelt thanks, and that you know how important you are to me. And I also hope you know that these are not just some more pretty words. They are words sent from my heart to you, Mother, to say how very much I love you.

— Donna Fargo

Thanks to you, Mom...

I *can look back on my childhood and realize how lucky I was to have you as a mother.*

I had some of the happiest birthdays, holidays, and family vacations that any child ever had. No matter how many years pass, I find that these memories never fade. They always shine brightly in my heart.

I also grew up knowing I was cared about and loved. Now, no matter what I encounter in my life, I'm always full of confidence and hope – because I know how much you believe in me.

I always knew that I could find safety and comfort in your loving arms, hope and strength in your caring heart, acceptance and love in your beautiful smile. And that's still true today.

I did not always realize all of these things when I was younger – at least not in ways that I could put into words. So I want to tell you now how wonderful it is to have you in my life: the best mom there could ever be.

– Edmund O'Neill

What Is a Family?

*A family is a home within the heart.
It's the place where love starts
and never ends; it's the place
where happiness begins.*

*A family is a blend of people
and personalities who share a common
path on their travels through this world.
Under one roof and enfolded within one
wonderful feeling, a family brings together
a million memories of yesterday and a
dream that distant tomorrows will keep
them close, no matter what.*

*A family is acceptance. A family is trust.
A family is understanding when
   no one else is.
A family is perseverance and deep,
   personal pride.
Nothing can compare to the bond they share,
to the history they hold within, or to the way
their lives are interwoven with every smile,
every tear, and every meaningful moment in
the years they spend together. Other things
may come and go, but a family
   will never be apart.*

*A family is a home... warm within
   the heart.*

— Collin McCarty

You Are the Most Important
and Beautiful Person in Our Family

*T*hank you for providing us
   with the stability
to keep us confident
the knowledge to help us
   accomplish things
the strength to help us
   conquer difficulties
the dedication to help
   us grow
and the enormous amount of time
   that you spend
to keep us close
Thank you
for always being there to help
for always being there
   to understand
and for always being there
   to care
You are a very rare person
because you put your family's needs
   far ahead of your own

I want you to know
how much I appreciate this
I want to thank you
for being such an important
    and beautiful person
in our family
and I want you to know
    that you can
depend on me
for anything that you might need
I love you more
than anything in the world

– Susan Polis Schutz

You have given me so many gifts
   over the years,
but the most important ones
were not covered in colorful paper
or given on special occasions.
You have given me
the wonderful gift of laughter;
I remember so many times
when we all laughed so hard.
You have given me the gift of sensitivity;
because of you, I learned to be
aware of the needs of others
and to help whenever I am able.
You have given me the gift of honesty;
you stressed the importance of being truthful
with others as well as with myself.
Your gift of faith is a treasure
hard to find in today's world;
I was fortunate to have you
show me its importance.
You have always loved me so openly
   and warmly,
and, thanks to you, I am able
to reach out to others and touch
their lives in a meaningful way.
I am able to hug, to hold, and
to express my love to those close to me.
It's these and all your countless gifts that
have made me especially grateful
for a mom like you.

— Chris Ardis

These Are the Gifts
I Would Like to Give to You

A heartfelt thank-you... *for all the things you do for me* ⋆ My assurance... *that I really <u>do</u> remember the things you taught me, and I always will* ⋆ Plenty of reasons... *for you to feel proud of me, which I'll achieve by always striving to be and do my best* ⋆ A sincere apology... *for any headaches I may have caused you when I was growing up* ⋆ A gift certificate... *to be redeemed anytime – as many times as you want – for anything I can ever do for you* ⋆ My promise... *that no matter how far away from home I may travel, you are never far from my heart* ⋆ My continued commitment... *to our family and the values you have taught me* ⋆ Recognition... *for all the great things you've done in your life (not the least of which was me!)* ⋆ An invitation... *to always be a part of my life, and to never feel that you have to ask* ⋆ A bunch of wishes... *that you have the peace, joy, and happiness in your life, which you are so deserving of* ⋆ My love... *forever and always.*

– Anna Marie Edwards

As I Have Grown, So Have My Appreciation and Love for You

"*T*ime flies," everyone says.
It's frightening sometimes
to look in the mirror and see
the evidence of that.
So often, we don't take a moment
    to say what's in our hearts,
and then, when it's too late,
    we wish we had.
I'm taking a moment now, Mom,
to tell you this...
When I was a child, there was
so much I couldn't understand,
like how hard you worked
and how much you sacrificed
    for our family.
There were dreams you had
    to put on hold
and dreams that never came true.

You must have felt frustrated
   sometimes, no doubt,
and at times even full of despair.
Yet you never gave less
   than your best to us.
You didn't have an exciting career
   or beautiful clothes.
You never traveled the world
   or drove a fancy car.
Every day, you looked after us,
   worried about us, fed us,
      and loved us,
without expecting anything in return.
You see, Mom, I know now
   and understand
that you actually gave me two lives:
my own... and yours.

                    – Cheryl Van Gieson

If They Gave Out Prizes for "Most Special Person of the Year"...

I want you to know
that my vote would
   surely go to you, Mom.

If the judges asked
for the reasons why,
I'd tell them I could answer
with a list a thousand pages long
about why you're so wonderful to me.

And there would be no question;
   you would be
   the winner in my book...
      definitely.

– Carey Martin

Dear Mom,

I used to express how much I loved you by holding out my arms and saying, "This much," or by bringing you big dandelion bouquets or crumpled crayon drawings, or by planting sticky kisses on your face. When you're a kid, it's so easy to show what's in your heart.

But as the years went by, I looked for other ways and means to show my love. I wanted to vividly express how much was in my heart; I wanted to say thank you for everything and let you know how much you mean to me; I wanted you to realize that I've matured to the point of being able to openly convey my deepest feelings for you... but I've found that words alone are never enough.

So, I hope you can picture me, holding out my arms and saying, "I love you... THIS MUCH!" because I can't think of any better way of expressing all that's in my heart for you.

– Barbara J. Hall

Mother, I Remember...

I remember when I was young and
would snuggle under my blanket; you
always tucked me in with a hug and a
kiss and words that reassured me of your
love. I remember how safe and secure
I felt when I closed my eyes to sleep.
I remember when I awoke in the morning
and you were always there waiting with
a smile on your face, preparing my favorite
breakfast. I remember you standing there
waving good-bye as I walked off to school.
I remember your words of wisdom and
encouragement when I faltered and was
afraid to try my wings at something new.
I remember the look of worry on your face,
although you tried to hide it well.
I remember how special you made all the
holidays with your decorations, and how you
would cook for days to prepare our favorite
recipes for family gatherings as you hummed
seasonal songs. I remember how I wanted
those days to last forever.

*I remember when I decided to venture out
on my own; you pushed me gently rather than
show your pain and anxiety. I remember you
standing there waving good-bye as I
wandered off to face the world.
I remember your smile, your gentle voice,
the warmth I felt in your arms, and all that
you gave of yourself to those you love.
I remember every day how fortunate I am
that you are my mother.*

And I always remember how much I love you!

– Geri Danks

Mom, I'll Always Be Your Child at Heart

Sometimes I wish I were still a child held tightly in your arms – sharing all my dreams, confessing all my fears, and knowing that you'll always be able to make my troubles disappear.

I can't remember exactly when it started... but the older I grew, the more I wanted to keep things to myself. So I wouldn't tell you my feelings; I tried not to show my pain. Yet somehow you always knew and understood the way that I am.

You've always been able to sense my pain, interpret my feelings, and comfort me with your caring ways. Most important of all, you have allowed me the privacy of my thoughts and my sense of independence – empowering me to grow as a person and as an adult.

I want you to know now how much I love you, and how much your love means to me. You have always been there for me.

If any love on earth is selfless, I know it's your love for me. This thought has helped me through so many difficult times when I was alone and wondering if anyone cared.

I sometimes long for those days when I was a child, embraced in your arms. But underneath the maturity I try to convey and the emotional security that I seek in the self-reliant lifestyle I've tried to establish for myself... I'll always be a child at heart, and I will always need you!

– Lan T. Nguyen

Thank You, Mom

I want to apologize
for any problems
that I may have caused you
in the past
I am not
the easiest person
to live with
since I am so
independent and strong
but you can be sure
that though it possibly
didn't seem like it
your values and ideals
did pass on to me
and I carry them forward
in all that I do

You always were someone
stable, strong, giving and warm
an ideal person to look up to
This has given me the
strength to lead
my own life
according to my own standards
Your leadership and love
have enabled me to grow
into a very
happy person
and I think that is
what every mother wishes
for her child
Thank you

– Susan Polis Schutz

Being a Mom Is
the Greatest Job in the World

*W*here else can you get a bonus paid in hugs and kisses? Of course, the salary isn't the greatest, but you're always assured of steady work.

Being a mom calls for the most diverse qualifications. Teacher (for homework); chauffeur (for carpool); maid (for picking up messes); minister (to give those much-needed sermons); doctor (for skinned knees); therapist (to dispense unsolicited advice); parole officer (for being grounded).

What other job description could offer so many challenging opportunities? And the greatest perk of all is job security – you don't have to worry about downsizing or layoffs! A good mom is hard to find.

– Connie Meyer

A Mother's Heart

There is a certain magic that happens
when a woman becomes a mother.
From the first joyful moment she holds
    her newborn child,
an amazing transformation
    begins to take place.
Nourished by a fountain of unconditional love,
her heart fills and expands and strengthens
to nurture and protect her child
    for time eternal.
In a mother's heart, no child is ordinary;
she sees the beauty a hasty world often ignores.
A mother's heart feels her offspring's pain,
and she is always there with words
    of encouragement.
A mother's heart never gives up.
No matter how cold or dark life seems,
no matter what others may think,
no matter how many obstacles are in her path,
she never loses hope and faith in her child.
No matter how far we go or how much we achieve,
few accomplishments in life are as rewarding
as a single smile from a mother's heart.

– Patricia A. Teckelt

There are some things
that I've always
meant to tell you.
So if you have a minute or two,
here are a few things
I just need to say...

Thank you, Mom, for choosing to give me life,
*   for wanting me, and for loving me.*
Thank you for taking care of me
*   through all my childhood illnesses*
*   (even when I made some of them up).*
Thank you for bandaging my scraped knees,
*   cut fingers, and wounded heart.*
You'll never know how grateful I am
*   for all those hot, home-cooked meals*
*   and midnight talks over hot chocolate.*

Thank you for helping me grow,
  for allowing me to try my wings,
  and for never saying, "I told you so,"
  when some of my flights had rough landings.
Thank you for always cheering me on
  and for having confidence in me,
  even when I had none in myself.
Thank you for showing you were proud of me,
  no matter how small the accomplishment.

There just aren't enough words
  to tell you all the feelings in my heart.
I know these aren't the most eloquent,
  but more than anything I want to say,
"Thank you for being the best mom
  anyone could ever have."

                            – Janet Kostelecky Nieto

May you be surrounded
   by the best today,
for that's the way this world
should always be for you.
May your day be bright
   and shining with
the sun's warmest golden rays.
May today be woven with
   the colors of the rainbow,
filled with promise,
happy, serene,
and so perfect
that it can't be interrupted
except to grow better
minute by minute, hour by hour.
Today, may you take these wishes
   into your heart
as gifts that mine is sending
   to yours.
And may life's blessings
appear for you today
and every day of the year.

— Barbara J. Hall

"Forever"

Forever is how long I'm going to love you, Mom. It's a word to let you know how long I'll care. Beyond every season. Past every sunrise. Each moment of my life. In whatever tomorrow holds, you will be held by me. Warm within my heart. Sweetest of all my memories.

Forever is a way of saying how long I'll be thanking you for being such a beautiful inspiration to me; for being so strong, for being so wise... for being the one woman I would have chosen so gratefully as my mother... if the choice had been up to me.

*Forever is for always.
Through whatever comes along.*

*Whenever my heart is overflowing with
gratitude, admiration, and love...
I always know that it's because
I've been thinking of you, Mom.*

– Laurel Atherton

My Perfect Mother

Your heart is big. Your love is pure. You want the best for me and care about everything I'm going through. You often put my needs above your own and overlook my mistakes. You love me without condition. Whatever I am and whatever I do is okay with you. You accept me... all of me. You're more than I could have ever hoped for in a mother. You're my perfect mother, and I'm so thankful for you.

You're always there: to hear my complaints, to share my joy, to feel my pain, to listen to my latest adventure, to advise me, to cry with me and hope for me and laugh with me, to forgive me when I do something dumb. I've never heard a harsh word from you that wasn't justified. I've never seen selfishness from you... only a mother who gives her love freely, happily, joyfully, and perfectly.

If I looked the world over, I could never find a mother more perfect than you. If I could choose anyone at all for my mom, I'd choose you. I'm so lucky that God put me in your family and gave me you for a mother. After all, I wouldn't be me without you. You're my perfect mother, and I love you and appreciate you more than I could ever express. I hope and pray that you're happy and that your every dream comes true. I pray for your perfect health and unlimited joy.

– Donna Fargo

Mom...

We have had difficult times
in our relationship –
times when our strong wills
overshadowed the love in our hearts.
Sometimes I chose a different path
than you wanted me to,
yet you were always there to show me
the way back home
and to welcome me
into your comforting arms.
It has taken me a while
to appreciate your wisdom;
I had to first stop looking at you
through the eyes of a child.
Now I want to tell you
what I haven't told you often enough...

I love you,
and I'm so happy
that you are
my mother.

– Lori Glover

It takes a special woman
to rise to the challenges
of being a mom.
It takes a positive attitude
to remain optimistic
when the going gets rough.
Being a mom takes
a lot of self-confidence
to stand strong
when it would be so much easier
just to give in.
It takes belief in yourself
and your family
to find the power to work
toward a better day.
It takes tenderness of spirit
and gentleness of heart
to respond to life's
day-to-day changes,
with your total concentration
focused on one thing:
the health and well-being
of your family.
Being a mom
takes a woman who has
a unique way of transforming
life's difficult moments
into love's greatest memories.
It takes a wonderful mother
like you.

– Linda E. Knight

Ten Absolutely
Wonderful Things
About Mothers

1.   *Mothers deserve the moon and the stars in return for all the things they are.*

2.   *Mothers are living proof that some things are priceless and some miracles really do come true.*

3.   *No matter how hectic things may get, mothers are always there for you. Even when it seems like there's no time left, they make time – for the things they do.*

4.   *Mothers go a million miles out of their way.*

5.   *They deserve more than the wealthiest person on earth could ever begin to repay.*

6. No one can make rainbows out of the rain like a mother can.

7. Mothers are a smile that stays inside you, and a hand that is always holding your hand.

8. When you've made a mistake, no matter how big it's been, a mother's arms always open wide enough to take you in.

9. A mother is a remarkable blending of beautiful thoughts and precious memories, the dearest of all people...
    and the best of all friends.

10. A mother is what happiness is all about. She is sweetness that comes into your life the day you are born and that never – ever – ends.

– Collin McCarty

I Know It Isn't Always Easy Being My Mom

I always feel so good about having
   someone as wonderful as you
      as my very own mother.

But there are times when
   I feel badly about the things
      I put you through.

Mom, I don't mean to make
   things difficult for you.

I don't mean to do anything that
upsets you or makes you worry about me.
But I know that there are times
   when I haven't been all I should be.
I know that you care so much
   because you love me.
And because you only want what's best.

So let me just tell you how sorry I am
for any time I've ever let you down.
And let me thank you for bringing me up
   in the sweetest and most caring way
anyone ever could.

— Barin Taylor

Just a Reminder...
Mom, I Love You

We don't talk a lot
about our feelings
for each other.
We show it in other ways –
by our enjoyment and laughter
when we're together,
by helping one another,
and by listening and caring.
Ever since I was born,
you've been demonstrating love
that is complete
and unconditional.
So I want you to know
that though I don't get
many chances to prove
my love for you,
it is there just the same –
constant and pure,
complete and unconditional,
just like yours.
I know I don't always
make that clear,
and I don't want there
to be any doubt.
So remember that I love you;
I always have,
and I always will.

– Barbara Cage

Mom, You Are My Inspiration and My Strength

I *have always admired your strength.*
In moments of crisis,
when the family seemed to be
* falling apart,*
you would know exactly what to do
* to make things right.*
I have watched while you
* allowed me and others*
to lean on you during
* those difficult times.*
You were there to celebrate
* the joyous times, too –*
showing your love with hugs
* and praise,*
so proud of our achievements.

I am honored that you are my mother
and I am blessed to have shared
my life with you.
I have learned from you how to be
loving and dependable.
Because of you, I know the comfort
of having someone I believe in
  so much
that I can go to her
to help bear my burdens
and share my troubles.
You have given so much of yourself
  to me,
and I too have some of your strength –
the special kind that emerges
when a person is strong enough
to be vulnerable to the people
they love.
I want you to know that
if you ever need me,
I will be there for you,
because I love you with all my heart.

– Lori Pike

You Are the Heart of Our Home and Family

I don't know how you did it, Mom...
but somehow, you were able to take
your love and commitment to
*   being a mother*
and blend it together with
thousands of bedtime stories,
dozens of holidays and birthday celebrations,
and a million memories
to create the best place on earth
for any child to grow up in:

*   our home.*

For the rest of my days,
I will strive to fulfill
the values and dreams
*   you inspired in me.*
And with love and pride, I will
*   always hold you in a special place:*

*   the home you have*
*   within my heart.*

– Edmund O'Neill

In Our Home...

We will not only talk, we will listen.
We will not only understand,
    we will communicate.
We will have a healthy set of values
    and believe in them
with a conviction that can be passed on
from generation to generation.
We will be expressive, not only with our love
    for one another
but with our forgiveness as well.
We will teach by our actions.
We will encourage and support.
We will respect one another's views
    as well as their privacy.
We will be there in a crisis.
We will rebuild in times of adversity,
    and when a problem arises
we will settle it together.
We will have a sense of humor,
    and take time to laugh and play
    as well as work together.
We will treat others fairly and justly,
    and expect the same in return.
We will seek to set an example,
    not just so others will want
to follow in our footsteps,
but so they will know that
our home is a place where love lives.

– Linda E. Knight

Thank You for
Always Encouraging Me
to Be the Best I Can

*M*om, I wish I could find a way
to let you know how important you are
and how much I respect you.
I will always be grateful to you
for being there
    and showing me
        what truly matters.
If I have failed to
learn the lessons you taught me,
it is not due to
a lack of encouragement from you,
but a lack of understanding
and appreciation
    on my part.

As my priorities change
and develop,
I find myself looking
for direction
from someone who has given me
    more than I deserve.
You have been the one
who stood behind me
in every way,
the one who pointed me forward,
nudged me on,
and the one who has shown me
that life is to be taken
for what it is
and made into something grand.
All that I am today, I owe to you.
I hope I can make you
as proud of me
as I am to have someone like you
for my mother.

– Carrie Rowe

*So many times, I think of myself
as a strong and independent person,
filled with confidence and pride.
And sometimes I forget that...*

It's All Because
of You, Mom...

*If I'm strong, it's because
you've shown me how to handle
problems without being overwhelmed
by them.
If I'm gentle, it's because you held
me close when I was sad and quietly
waited with me while life leveled out.
If I use my sense of humor, it's
because you've taught me to laugh
and keep life's challenges in
perspective.*

If I'm independent and confident,
it's because you let me know it
was all right to have my own
thoughts and make my own choices.
If I'm compassionate, it's because
you have shown me the importance
of caring about people rather
than possessions.
If I'm loving and passionate, it's
because you have shown me your love
through all the ups and downs of
growing up and growing away.

I'll try never to forget
that the best parts of me
are from you.
Thanks.

– Judith Hintz Tanaka

All of My Life, Mom...

I've stood a little taller,
walked a little prouder,
and felt a little safer
when I was afraid.
I have laughed a little harder,
cried a whole lot less,
and found my way
in a confusing world.
I have tried things
I never would have otherwise,
accomplished more than
I thought possible,
and grown stronger
in your warm embrace.

Life has gone a little smoother,
fears passed a little quicker,
and my dreams became realities.
I have learned to think
with an open mind,
respect my own opinions,
welcome new challenges,
and believe in myself...

because you are my mom.

— Donna L. West

Thank You for Being So Nice

I am wondering if anyone
has taken the time to
thank you for being so nice
You are a rare person
You are always so considerate of people –
putting their needs in front of yours
You are always so kind –
treating people in such a caring way
If everyone were like you
the world would be so peaceful
Though people are often too busy
to stop and thank you
I hope you can feel the respect and love
that everyone has for you
And though many times
I have wanted to thank you
I never got around to it
So right now
I want to emphasize my thanks to you
for being such a
wonderful person

– Susan Polis Schutz

A Loving Tribute
to My Mother

In my mother's hands, I see
   all of the hard work
that she has done for me.
I see the caring they've provided
   for my benefit
down through the years.

In my mother's eyes, I sense
   a gentle understanding
of my ways –
and also a longing to sometimes
   help me see some better ways
of living.

In my mother's arms, I've found
   comfort from the world
so many times –
from fears, hurts, and everything
   that troubles me.
I know that if anything happens
   to bother me now,
those arms are always open
   just for me.

In my mother's face, I see
the hopes for me
that are plainly written there;
often, a sense of pride
is revealed, too.

But in my mother's heart
is the greatest gift of all,
for that is where so much love
is kept for me.

– Barbara J. Hall

As a child
held close in your arms,
I was safe, I was loved.
My first stumbling steps were taken
while tightly clasping your hand.
When I was brave enough
to step out on my own,
your praise and encouragement were there,
as were your arms
to pick me up when I fell.
First day of school. First bike ride.
First date. First heartache.
First love. First heartbreak.
All the firsts of a lifetime...
and you were there.
Somehow you always knew when to praise,
when to reassure, when to help me up,
and when to let me get up on my own.
In my mind, I can hear the echo of
your voice through the years.
In my memory, you smile.
I close my eyes and can feel
your loving arms.
You are ever near me.
Held close in your heart,
I am still safe, I am still loved.
And I love you
more than words can say.

– Mary George

Our Relationship
Is So Special to Me

I *hope that you know*
how very much I love you
and how much I appreciate
all that you have done for me.

I'm glad that we can be
open and honest with each other,
and I'm thankful that
there's nothing we can't talk about.

I'm glad that you've loved me enough
to let me choose my own dreams,
and I'm thankful that
you've offered me understanding
when I've made mistakes.

I'm glad that you've loved me enough
to allow me the room I need to grow,
and I'm thankful that
we've grown closer.

I'm glad that we have such a
loving relationship,
and I'm thankful that you are my mother.

– Donna Newman

*A day doesn't go by that
I don't realize how fortunate I am
    to be a part of our family.
I know our family isn't perfect,
and most likely, we never will be,
but we are a loving, caring family.
We've had our highs and lows.
We've been through some tough times
and had our share of easy times, too.
But we've always shared a sense of security
that has helped us through.
We've disagreed with each other
and even disappointed each other,
but we accepted those times of irritation,
knowing they would pass and we'd all come
to understand how each of us really felt.
Knowing that I could count on you,
no matter what, has made
the biggest difference in my life.*

I've always known that I had somewhere
I could go any time I needed help or guidance,
and I'd be welcome.
Thank you for the love you gave to me
and for the feelings of faith and trust.
You are a really incredible mom
who has made being a family
one of the best parts of my life.
No matter what life brings my way
or how my life changes from year to year,
I will always have love in my heart
and the feelings of family
to make my life worthwhile.

– Ben Daniels

The Love Between
a Mother and Child
Is Forever

*The love we share
as mother and child
is a bond of the strongest kind.
It is a love of the present,
interwoven with memories
of the past
and dreams of the future.
It is strengthened by overcoming
obstacles
and facing fears and challenges
together.
It is having pride in each other
and knowing that our love
can withstand anything.*

It is sacrifice and tears,
laughter and hugs.
It is understanding, patience,
and believing in each other.
It is wanting only the best
for each other
and wanting to help any time
there is a need.
It is respect, a hug,
and unexpected kindness.
It is making time to be together
and knowing just what to do and say.
It is an unconditional,
forever kind of love.

– Barbara Cage

I Have So Much Love in My Heart for You

I have in my heart
    the tears you cried with me,
    both silently and aloud.
I have in my heart
    the laughter you taught me to laugh,
    so that I would not take the world
    or myself too seriously.
I have in my heart
    the sacrifices you made for me,
    so that I might be happy.
I have in my heart
    the special things a mother says
    to her child.
I have in my heart
    the patience and understanding
    you showed me, so that I could
    see things through different eyes.
I have in my heart
    the courage you instilled in me
    to be myself and to soar
    with the wings you taught me to use.
I have in my heart so much
    love for you –
    my wonderful, beautiful,
        funny mother...
    love that you taught me
        just by being there.

– Claudine Krovoza

"I Love You, Mom"

There have been many times
   when I have missed the chance
   to tell you that I'm so proud
   of you and all you stand for.
I respect your discipline,
   your decisions, and the way
   you stand by your words.
I admire everything about your
   way of life, even though you
   may have wondered many times
   if I was even listening when
   you spoke to me.
You may have felt as if your words
   were falling on closed ears,
   but I've always heard you.
And many times those messages of
   yours have helped me, guided me,
   and kept me safely going on.

"Thanks, Mom"...
That's another phrase I haven't
   offered you as often as
   I should have.
If I did, I'd be saying those
   two words continually for
   everything you do for me.

But today, I'll just say,
   "I love you, Mom...
      You're always in my heart."

– Barbara J. Hall

ACKNOWLEDGMENTS

The following is a partial list of authors whom the publisher especially wishes to thank for permission to reprint their works.

PrimaDonna Entertainment Corp. for "You've Done So Much for Me... How Can I Ever Thank You?" by Donna Fargo. Copyright © 1997 by PrimaDonna Entertainment Corp. And for "My Perfect Mother," by Donna Fargo. Copyright © 1998 by PrimaDonna Entertainment Corp. All rights reserved. Reprinted by permission.

Barbara J. Hall for "Dear Mom." Copyright © 1997 by Barbara J. Hall. All rights reserved. Reprinted by permission.

Geri Danks for "Mother, I Remember...." Copyright © 1997 by Geri Danks. All rights reserved. Reprinted by permission.

Lan T. Nguyen for "Mom, I'll Always Be Your Child at Heart." Copyright © 1997 by Lan T. Nguyen. All rights reserved. Reprinted by permission.

Connie Meyer for "Being a Mom Is the Greatest Job in the World." Copyright © 1998 by Connie Meyer. All rights reserved. Reprinted by permission.

Patricia A. Teckelt for "A Mother's Heart." Copyright © 1998 by Patricia A. Teckelt. All rights reserved. Reprinted by permission.

Barbara Cage for "Just a Reminder... Mom, I Love You." Copyright © 1997 by Barbara Cage. All rights reserved. Reprinted by permission.

Lori Pike for "Mom, You Are My Inspiration and My Strength." Copyright © 1997 by Lori Pike. All rights reserved. Reprinted by permission.

Linda E. Knight for "In Our Home...." Copyright © 1997 by Linda E. Knight. All rights reserved. Reprinted by permission.

Mary George for "As a child held close in your arms...." Copyright © 1997 by Mary George. All rights reserved. Reprinted by permission.

A careful effort has been made to trace the ownership of poems used in this anthology in order to obtain permission to reprint copyrighted materials and give proper credit to the copyright owners. If any error or omission has occurred, it is completely inadvertent, and we would like to make corrections in future editions provided that written notification is made to the publisher:

BLUE MOUNTAIN PRESS, INC.,
P.O. Box 4549, Boulder, Colorado 80306.